GINNY'S GUIDE
TO A
DOG'S LIFE

GINNY'S GUIDE
TO A DOG'S LIFE

Over 60 top tips that guarantee treats

GINNY
with Chelsea England

DOG 'n' BONE

Published in 2014 by Dog 'n' Bone Books
An imprint of Ryland Peters & Small Ltd

20–21 Jockey's Fields, London WC1R 4BW
519 Broadway, 5th Floor, New York, NY 10012

www.rylandpeters.com

10 9 8 7 6 5 4 3 2 1

Text © Chelsea England 2014
Design and photography © Dog 'n' Bone Books 2014

A CIP catalog record for this book is available from the
Library of Congress and the British Library.

ISBN: 978 1 909313 25 5

Printed in China

Design: Mark Latter
Photography: Chelsea England

For digital editions, visit
www.cicobooks.com/apps.php

CONTENTS

INTRODUCTION

Ginny is a wise yet chunky Jack Russell. She has a lot of knowledge and advice to share with her fellow dogs. Most of her words of wisdom are to do with napping, eating, looking sassy, and putting us humans in our place. That's because Ginny seems to think those are the only things that matter. Of course, being a dog Ginny is unable to use a computer, so it has been my duty as her inferior human owner to type out all of her life lessons. As a result, this book is written in Ginny's clearly superior point of view.

I apologize in advance if your dog turns into a cheeky, sassy, and lazy pooch after hearing about Ginny's way of doing things.

GINNY'S TIPS

DEALING WITH HUMANS

When a human returns home to a dog after being out, it's absolutely necessary to jump up and down in front of them. This isn't to show the human that you're happy to see them, but to see if they have brought anything to give you as an apology for daring to leave the house without you. If they have nothing of value, you must instantly stop jumping and proceed to give the human the silent treatment.

When a human catches you doing something you should not be doing—like trying to destroy the sofa—just give them a little over the shoulder "Oh hey there, of course I'm not being naughty you silly human, does this innocent face look like it ever does anything naughty?" look. It works about 99% of the time.

I recommend that all dogs perfect the "don't lie to me you stupid human" face. This sassy look of utter disbelief works well for dogs when their humans don't tell the truth about the quantity of treats left, or if they pretend to throw the tennis ball when really they still have it in their hand.

DEALING WITH HUMANS 11

If a human gets too close to one of your prized possessions, let them know. A simple poking out of the tongue should do the trick. Those humans need to know the number one rule: what's mine is mine and what's yours is also mine. So leave my stuff alone!

As well as poking your tongue out at humans, another way to show that you're not at all satisfied is to give them some serious stink eye. A combination of stink eye and poking your tongue out really shows a human that you're ticked off, especially when they are making you waste energy walking in a cold field.

I like to start each day by stretching—
I encourage all dogs to try it. I guarantee it will make your
body feel great and ready for the day of sleeping ahead.
I don't like to stretch without the help of the sofa though;
otherwise my chunky tummy gets in the way.

A DOG'S BODY

Always embrace scruffy fur. As
you know, the windswept look is
so totally in style now! Just beware
of those humans who try to brush
your fur when they notice how
scruffy it is. Sadly, they are
incapable of understanding
what constitutes a good look
for us dogs.

15

Baths and showers are a dog's ultimate enemy. I'm absolutely positive no pooch should ever have to be cleaned, no matter how badly those crazy humans think we smell. My advice to all breeds out there: always shake dirty bath water over your human while they're cleaning you—it shows them you're in control. And remember to bring a squeaky toy for moral support.

The tongue is a tricky thing to operate. I've given up trying to control mine and have decided just to let it go where it wants. The same rule applies to my luscious fur after I've woken up from a nap with a bad case of bed head: just let it go where it wants! As you're a dog, the chances are that you'll look totally adorable with a messed up 'do anyway.

Side eye is a brilliant skill to learn. I love being able to look to the left or right without having to move my head. It makes it easier for me to monitor a situation and determine whether it's worth my time and the effort of moving to be involved.

EXERCISE

The only clean water a dog should ever be near is the liquid they find in their water bowl. Oh, and a paddling pool full of cool water when it's really hot outside is also acceptable. As always, dress appropriately for the occasion. I wore my goggles here so I could belly flop into the pool safely.

No matter what's in your way, you can leap over it to get where you want. When it comes to bacon treats, I will jump over anything to get to it. If you're feeling lazy, just get your human to carry you over an obstacle. As you probably know, those humans are only there to take care of our every need.

I have never understood weightlifting; the only thing that should be lifted is food into a dog's mouth. I have kindly opened my mouth here to facilitate the process of having some treats hoisted into it.

When I finally decide to run quickly, I like to make myself as aerodynamic as possible so I can get to my destination faster. It's hard for me to be streamlined because I'm so chunky and fluffy, but I've found that just poking my tongue out really helps me cut through the air.

EXERCISE 21

RELAXING

It's always good to listen to music before you sleep, it really helps you relax! My human tries to tell me listening to commercials for doggy treats doesn't count as music. I don't care though, it's still awesome to listen to.

It can be tiring work for a dog being so adorable all the time. I struggle with tiredness brought on by extreme cuteness. My advice isn't to fight it, have a big yawn and fall asleep where and whenever you want to, but make sure there's a human nearby to cover you with a blanket.

I like having a teddy bear to sleep next to—it makes sleeping more comfortable. Of course, if a dog can acquire a bag of treats to sleep beside that would be even better, but for now I've settled for this teddy until my human sees sense and gives me the treats.

Occasionally, a dog will look a little less than glamorous while sleeping. It rarely happens, but if it does make sure you give your human some stink eye for photographing you when you're not at your best.

Don't eat bubbles! They may look fun and tasty, but if
you eat them you'll be burping bubbles for days. My
human says I'm weird for eating strange things, but what
can I say, I'm a foodie!

Humans can never give a dog enough food. I always complain to mine how unfair it is that humans can just take what they want to eat from the kitchen, but us dogs can't. I suggest that all dogs give their human an unsubtle hint that they want feeding... right now!

Stay hydrated! It's hard to enjoy a precious nap if you're thirsty, so always make sure you have a drink close by! Or simply steal some of your human's drink, like I'm doing here. It's my humans fault I drank her tea, she shouldn't have made it so delicious and easy to get to.

Sometimes humans don't know what us dogs think about, so it's best to show those foolish humans what's going on in our highly intellectual minds. I like to spend my days thinking of treats, so I'm showing my human that. I sometimes think about sleeping, too. If it's not food or sleep, then it's just not worth reflecting on!

Squeaky toys can be deceiving. I've just discovered that while this toy looks like a doughnut, it doesn't taste like a doughnut. My solution to dealing with disappointing squeaky toys? Destroy them, bury them in the garden, and demand your human gets you something better next time. Seriously, you humans need to step up your game when trying to please us dogs with squeaky toys.

TREATS

When your efforts to get treats from those humans fail, put on something cute and melt their hearts with your adorableness until they feed you! Seriously, those humans are so easy to get treats from.

I think those inferior humans don't do enough for dogs. When I get one treat it's nowhere near sufficient; I deserve to be getting 1,000! I propose that a foot half-raised, like in this picture, should be an international sign from dogs to all humans that they require a pile of treats at least to an equivalent height of the paw.

Not enough songs are dedicated to treats, so I've put on my snazzy glasses, found a guitar, and decided to write my own. Unfortunately, it's not going very well. The second I sing about treats I start drooling and begging for some. Like many rockstars, this addiction is really stifling my creativity. Curse you treats and your delicious, tempting ways!

Sticks, along with tennis balls, make brilliant fetching utensils. They're also a lot easier to destroy and chew up when you're bored of chasing after them.

I firmly believe it's vital that you show your human who is boss. In this photo, my silly human had just told me I wasn't allowed to play ball in the house. To teach her a lesson, I decided to put up a basketball net and gave her the "Yeah, that's right, there's nothing you can do about this" look.

It's good for a dog to find things to do to pass the time until a human
feeds you again. I tried to play some card games... but I couldn't
hold the cards... or read what was written on the cards... or know
any of the rules... or find anyone to play with.

Tennis balls, tails, and soccer balls are among some of the things acceptable for a dog to chase. If you can persuade your human to not make you waste precious energy by playing chase that's a good thing. I couldn't convince my human, so I resorted to plan B: make her forget all about it with my cuteness and style.

Reading is an excellent way to gain knowledge, but unfortunately I don't know how to read. Instead I'll do the next best thing: sleeping. If snoozing were an Olympic sport, I'd be guaranteed to win gold.

THE GREAT OUTDOORS

A dog should always stare intently at things found outside, just in case the item they are looking at is edible or about to play chase. I'm focusing on grass here, but not to see if I could eat it or if it was about to break into a run. I was just trying to waste time on our walk so my human would pick me up and carry me home.

I love nature; it's something every dog should take more time to appreciate! Especially flowers, I love the smell of them. However, sometimes flowers get stuck to my nose and it takes an inferior human to get them off for me. If a human isn't there to remove the culprit from my nose, then I'll take it upon myself to try to eat it.

When I'm forced to go outside and actually make it further than 10 paces, I like to wear exercise-appropriate clothing. Us dogs have to look good no matter what we're doing, even if it is having to exercise against our will.

Outside you can always find great things to roll around in or run through—grass cuttings are my personal favorite. It's a dog's right to be able to roll in something that they think smells good. My human wasn't too pleased with this though; it took her ages to brush all the grass off of my face.

While walking through long grass, I would advise you to always stay close to your human. Not for safety reasons, just stay near them so they can pick you up and carry you when you're bored with walking through silly long grass. Humans make great forms of transport when you're tired.

WHATEVER THE WEATHER

Always dress appropriately for the weather. If the sun is shining, then a cap and sunglasses can help you a lot. On a related note, don't I look totally fabulous in this outfit? I know, I don't think there's an item of clothing that wouldn't suit me!

Due to the fact I have paws instead of hands (serious flaw there, if I had hands I could easily open the treat jar!), I can't make snowballs. But that doesn't stop me from getting covered in snow then shaking it off onto nearby humans. They act like they don't love it, but I know they do really. Avoid the yellow snow though, chances are I made it.

Snow greatly displeases me; as a well pampered dog I see no need to have to walk in the cold stuff. If something disappoints a dog then they must let their human know. This is why I'm poking my tongue out to demonstate I'm not very impressed at being made to suffer these conditions.

When it's hot outside and those silly humans insist on going for a walk, just sit in the middle of the path and adopt a pose so charming that it will make them forget about exercise. Using cuteness against humans is a dog's best skill.

If it's cold outside and the crazy humans still insist on taking you out, insist that you're given the time to dress warmly. Make sure you have also perfected the "You better take me home right now human, otherwise you'll be sorry" look. My human is lucky that pink is totally my color, so wearing that coat wasn't too bad.

CLOTHES

A girl can never have too many clothes; I'm always accessorizing and looking stylish.
I'm a fan of cozy garments; if I can't comfortably sleep in it then I don't want to wear it.

Human clothes are possibly the most awesome things to rest in. By now you're probably realizing that I think anything a human owns should belong to their dog instead, that includes hoodies. If it's agreeable to a dog, then that dog has the right to take it.

It may be good to be stylish, but don't be afraid to wear relaxing clothes, too. I like stealing my human's robe because it's the most wonderful thing—the Egyptian cotton feels great against my fur. It's also fun to see her get annoyed when an item looks better on a dog. What can I say, I just look good in everything!

Wearing glasses can make you appear really intelligent and professional. Sticking your tongue out, however, just makes you look sassy. So doing both together gives you the perfect mix of intelligence and sassiness. Also, when humans see you with your tongue out they think it's cute and give you treats— it's a win-win situation.

One of my favorite things to do is boss humans around, it's a well-known fact dogs are superior to them. It's important that a dog shows its inferior human owner who has authority, which is why I have dressed as a sheriff. I'm annoyed with my human for not getting me a sheriff's badge though, that would have made me look really snazzy.

FANCY DRESS

A dog should master the art of disguise, so that after a human gives you a treat you can put on a disguise, then go back for more because those silly humans won't recognize you. I bet you can't even tell it's me in this photo! That's just how well it works.

When I want to escape from my humans for a while, I wear this outfit and go and hide in the flowerbeds. It's so funny to watch them try to find me, particularly when they are just about to leave the house.

I'm not just adorable and lazy, I'm also a rebel without a cause that isn't scared to take treats from humans. Every rebel needs a big motorcycle to ride, but I couldn't find one so I'm using this child's trike. It doesn't have quite the same rebel look as a motorcycle, but I don't care because riding this trike means I don't have to waste energy walking. Besides, I'll probably get my human to chauffeur me around anyway.

CLASS, STYLE, AND SASSINESS

I like to dress classy to enjoy a meal. No matter what's being served, dressing well makes it better. Unless, of course, you're being given low-fat dog food; nothing makes that stuff taste good.

Class is important. A classy exterior leads to a classy interior, so always keep up appearances. Having said that, my human tells me wearing a suit and tie then burping isn't classy, but we all know she's wrong—it's the height of class!

When you look classy humans respect you and feed you more. If you can master a sophisticated look to go with your stylish dress code, then those humans will never be able to say no to you.

Us dogs have to be sassy sometimes. Occasionally dogs have to raise their paw and tell the humans "talk to the paw, because the face isn't listening. Unless you have treats, then I'm all ears!"

If you can't dress classy, at least dress like you know
what you're doing. I have no idea about anything
unless it's sleeping or food, but when I look like this,
people think I know absolutely everything.

HEALTH AND BEAUTY

To stay looking young and beautiful, a dog should regularly have mud baths. For some reason, humans don't seem very happy when a dog comes back covered in mud. They just don't understand the hard work it takes for a pup to stay looking so gorgeous.

Bed head is something that can't be avoided, but for some reason all dogs look spiffing with messy fur. After all, bed head is a sign that a dog has been busy getting precious sleep, which is always good.

My human calls this fur style messy; I prefer the term "out of control fluffiness." Humans never understand how much effort it takes to get our fur like this. One thing my human does agree on is that I still look adorable like this.

HARD AT WORK

I'm very tech savvy, I like to check my emails and make sure all of my online treat deals are going well. Occasionally I'll get distracted by online videos of cats, but when I'm not watching those, I'm always hard at work. One piece of advice: you may have to employ a human to type for you, our lack of thumbs doesn't make it easy... that and the fact we can't read.

Dress for the job you want, not the job you have! Like right here, I'm dressed as Batman because I want to be a superhero. Other jobs I am interested in are: professional napper, professional eater and a professor in anything to do with bacon.

When a human catches you next to a hole in the back yard, deny that you did it. Blame it on cats if you have to. However, if the human likes the job you've done, then by all means admit to your handiwork. After all, you might get a treat out of it. Sadly, I've rarely heard of such a thing happening.

Humans don't seem to appreciate it when a dog does a spot of excavation. I've never understood why, but I have discovered the next best thing to do instead of digging holes with my paws is to get some proper gardening equipment and use that instead. My best soil-removing tip is for a dog to ignore a human when they tell you to stop it; they're just jealous of our wonderful digging skills.

ACKNOWLEDGMENTS

First of all, I would like to thank you, kind citizen, for buying this book. If you're at your friends house, they paid for it, and you're just looking at it, then this thank you isn't for you. Just kidding! I'll thank you as well for taking an interest in *Ginny's Guide To A Dog's Life*. So thanks to all the lovely people who buy this book, or even just have a quick flick through.

A huge thank you to everyone that follows Ginny's adventures online, your support and constant kind words mean the world to Ginny and I.

Thank you to Pete Jorgensen and all at Dog 'n' Bone Books for making this book possible.

Thank you to Lauren and Jesse at CrazyRebels.com for making Ginny look so stylish.

Thank you to my wonderful family for everything; you're an amazing bunch of people and a constant source of inspiration.

And lastly, even though she can't read this, thank you to Ginny for being a fluffy little hugging machine that makes me smile daily, even when she is being cheeky.